Cut From the Same Cloth

A Collection of Smith Family Stories

1841 – 2006

Family Edition

About the Author:

Cynthia's parents migrated, during the 1940s, moving from Texas to California, shortly after World War II. She was born in 1948, growing up in Berkeley, and Richmond, California. She came from a close-knit, hardworking family. She grew up hearing stories told by her mother about family members and of times long ago. She writes about the stories and about life in the little known, towns that were isolated communities cut off from mainstream society known only as sawmill towns.

Cynthia was educated in Northern California schools and local community colleges (Laney, Contra Costa and Solano). She describes herself as the "self-designated", family historian and photographer. Older family members from her father's side would bequeath to her family heirlooms, artifacts and photographs. She became intrigued by the people in the pictures, of places, of another time. Her love of books and the lifelong desire of owning a bookstore became a reality, during 1992-1996. Her tenure as a bookseller exposed her to the literary world of book fairs, author signings and of course, numerous books, especially history. She planned events for nationally known authors to book signings and other appearances; some were hosted by nearby Solano College. That exposure would prepare her for the next experience of her life, by adding to her desire to trace her family's history with the study of genealogy. Once retiring from her position as a Human Resources Administrator at a nearby health agency in 2005, she resumed researching her family's history. This time focusing on her mother's family and telling their story.

Cynthia's most notable accomplishments have been to add more branches to her family tree and as a dedicated genealogist; she currently provides beginner genealogy instruction and workshops at local libraries. One major accomplishment as a result of the workshops has been the formation of a local discussion group, the African American Genealogical Society of Solano County, established in March 2009, from participants of the workshops. The group provides workshops, guest speakers and seminars. The most recent inclusion into the African American Genealogical Society of Northern California, from the members of the discussion group, has broadened the opportunities and resources to all interested in researching family history. Cynthia resides in Fairfield, California.

Printed in the United States
By Bookmasters

A Gift For: _____

From: _____

"Arise, shine; for thy light is come and the glory of the Lord is risen upon thee."
Isaiah 60:1

Table of Contents

EMOTIONAL ENERGY

Emotional Energy was written to energize and uplift everyone spiritually through poetry, bible verses and images.

546382-Jonquille.
ISBN: Softcover 978-1-4257-6400-5
          Ebook   978-1-4771-8010-5

EMOTIONAL ENERGY
Energize your spirit

This book is dedicated to my mother, Marrie George, who is battling cancer at this time. It is my hope that these poems of inspiration may help you to overcome this disease. Thank you for always being my source of strength.

I would also like to say thank you to my Lord God, my husband Mark, family and friends for supporting and believing in me. To my brother Deion George for his inspiring and continued support. Also special thanks to Angelo Pearson, Lonnie Ollivierre, Nicole Pace, Aimee Miller, Chris Solan, Tre Sanders, Errol Tominlson, Tyrone Shorter, Edie Stahlberger and H. Mulgrave for their invaluable assistance in the preparation of this book and bringing my poems to life with such beautiful verses and paintings.

Introduction

Emotional Energy is a collection of approximately 25 poems that cover many facets of an individual's life, moving from the evils one faces to finally finding the answer. Jonquille also includes a spirit lifting testimonial, while other pieces reveal the harsher realities as well as joyful events in life. All poems include a bible verse as well as image to give everyone a different perspective on life.

So many of us have times when we're feeling down. Some of us complain of being spiritually or morally dead. We may have feelings of worthlessness, helplessness, guilt, and self blame. American psychologist Martin Seligman suggests that depression stems from "learned helplessness" an acquired belief that one cannot control the outcome of events. Lynn Abramson and her colleagues argue that depression results not only from helplessness, but also from hopelessness, a pattern of negative thinking.

Depression is a very serious problem and not to be taken lightly. When you are depressed, the past and the future are absorbed entirely by the present. This book in no way suggests that our poetry and images should replace professional treatment for a serious psychological condition. I encourage you to be patient and persistent, seek professional help.

For lighter forms of depression or a spiritual energy booster, a smile, or to encourage others, meditate on these poems. I believe that if we can genuinely wish ourselves happiness and radiate that wish to others, our mind can change dramatically. The most important thing to understand is that we can change our own mind if we make a bit of effort.

Dazzling

My colors are filled with joy,
exuberant and dazzling,
conditioned to elude you.

My sounds will hypnotize you, for I am that what you see,
a sultry songstress, captivating.

I am here to take control, control your life even your soul.
Watch for me,
I am live in livin color,

dangerous to the core.
Don't allow me to capture you, for I will persuade you.
For I am live in livin color

Seek good, not evil, that you may live. Then the Lord God Almighty
will be with you, just as you say he is.
Amos 5:15

I Am

Serwa, a blessed child of God. I am a beautiful golden flower, a loving energy, a spirit, a guardian angel to many.

I am Serwa, a blessed child of God.

I am a mother, a daughter, a sister, a wife a caretaker to all.

I am Serwa, a blessed child of God.

I am a student, a writer, a poet, an entrepreneur, an advisor for sure.

I am Serwa, a blessed child of God.

I am African, Indian, Latin, European, Asian. I am many formed as one. I am that which you seek, but hard to find.

I am, Serwa "A Royal Woman".

And God said unto Moses, I AM THAT I AM: and he said, Thus shalt thou say unto the children of Israel, I AM hath sent me unto you.
Exodus 3:14

Sister Friend

You're a rare find.
In my life's journey, I've adopted a few,
and among them,
I found you.

Independence and wisdom you have plenty.

I've seen your soul and felt your pain.
I've seen you cry, you may not have known.

I feel you my sister-friend, and will always be there for you.
You're beautiful and strong,
don't let anyone fool you.

Light the way sister-friend
your chariot awaits you.

Ointment and perfume rejoice the heart: so doth the sweetness of a
man's friend by hearty counsel.
Proverbs 27:9

11

Father and Son

Let me be that shoulder you lean on
Can't they understand that you're my little man

Let me make you smile instead of frown
For little do they know the power that grows
Our love is one without bottom

A yearning that lingers throughout the seasons

We are kings who rule from within
Stand up, be humble and face the struggle
My love is solid, unchanging
Such depth some folks can't fathom
Play your part as a strong man

For I am with you always now and beyond

My son, let not them depart from thine eyes: keep sound wisdom and discretion:
Proverbs 3:21

Precious moments in time

Lest we forget how precious life is

The birth of our child

Our first dance, kiss or first love

Let's not forget
Our child's smile, walk or talk

Our precious moments in time
For it is our most treasured

Whereas ye know not what shall be on the morrow. For what is your life? It
is even a vapour, that appeareth for a little time, and then vanisheth away.
James 4:14

Eze

I am Eze, a child of God. I am a man of principle,
a spiritually fulfilled soul, a positive force.

I am Eze, a child of God
I am a father, a son, a brother, a husband, a leader in my castle.
I am Eze, a child of God

I am enriched with wisdom, strength,

love and courage.

A lion in this harsh jungle.
I am Eze, a child of God

I am a proud African, Indian, Latin, European, Asian.

I am Ezeoha, a people's King I am here to keep you safe,
just reach out and allow me to be.

I am Eze, "King"

"He hath showed thee, O man, what is good; and doth the Lord require of
thee, but to do justly, and to love mercy, and to walk humbly with thy God?"
Micah 6: 8

Offering

I offer you
my hand, It may not look like much, but in this hand you'll find
warmth, comfort, experience, love
a way out.
Read me and follow my lines.
You may see my past, present and future,
a guide to lead you.
Take my hand, allow me to show you the way.
I offer you my hand.

"and has extended mercy to me before the king and his counselors, and before
all the king's mighty princes. So I was encouraged, as the hand of the Lord my
God was upon me; and I gathered leading men of Israel to go up with me".
Ezra 7:28

Seasons

We are like the seasons of Earth as they change so does the mind, body and
soul. Spring brings new birth, physically and spiritually,
as the circle of life begins a new journey.

Summer brings warmth, as we come out to play our true faces are seen.
Our souls may become lost, indulging in summer's heat.

Fall brings so many changes as we admire nature. Trees come alive with vibrancy.
The air is filled with pure bliss. We give thanks and cherish our blessings.

Winter, its beauty can be devastatingly alluring, a seducing vision of vibrant
sunshine. An inoculating fuse of purity and tainted ground, we become

unselfish, embracing our spirituality, we become enlightened beings.
As the seasons change we change.

We grow, we dream, we love we start over, and somewhere
inbetween, we recognize who we are.

While the earth remaineth, seedtime and harvest, and cold and heat, and
summer and winter, and day and night shall not cease.
Gen. 8:22

Rain

Rain, rain, rain

Rain down on me
Wash, cleanse me

Heal my soul

Hold me in your warm embrace
Cure and renew me

Touch my spirit

Fill me with sweet nature's water
Allow me to grow, soar
Rejuvenate my mind
Drench my spirit, soul, mind and body
So that I may run with you

Rain, rain, rain

Hide thy face from my sins, and blot out all mine iniquities. Create in me a clean heart, O God; and renew a right spirit within me. Cast me not away from thy presence; and take not thy holy spirit from me. Restore unto me the joy of thy salvation; and uphold me with thy free spirit.
Psalms 51:9-12

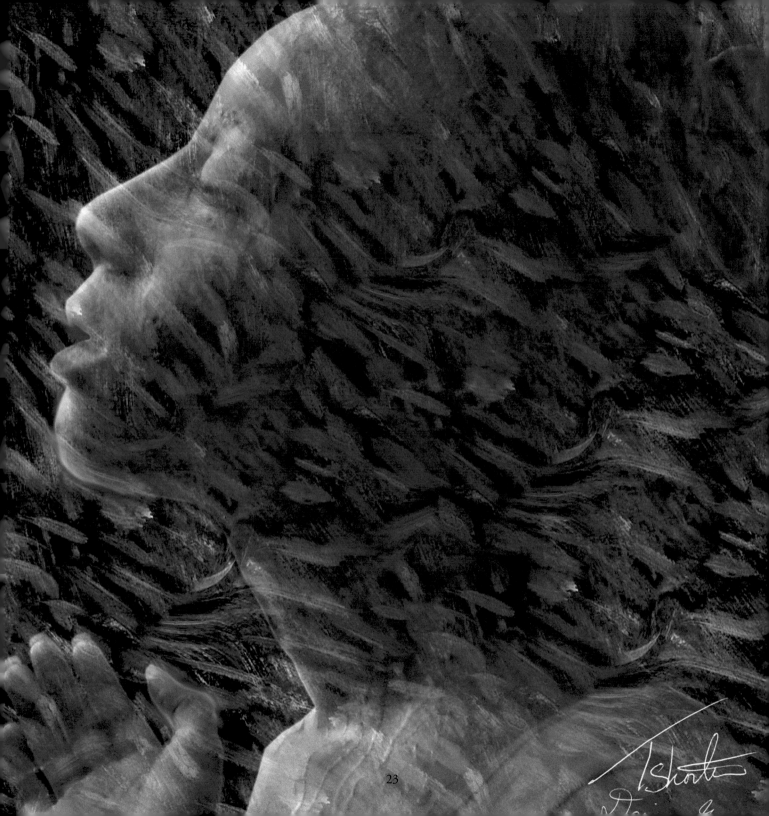

23

Sunrise

Have you ever watched the sun rise, as she starts the day.

How bright and optimistic she looks, so looking forward
to starting a new day.

Like the smile on my baby's face, when she wakes up in
the morning, just happy to see her mommy and daddy
smiling back at her secure.

And as time passes she greets each cloud and space in the
sky, leaving them with an inspiring color and message
to spread through the atmosphere. Whether it is to cleanse
the earth with rain and snow, or to brighten it and keep it

warm with her exuberant rays.

Oh how I love to watch her as she makes her journey

across the sky, facing the daily adventures of the earth as it changes.
Surviving to take her rest at the end of the day, sitting on the

ocean and beyond, resting to rise another day bright and
enthusiastic ready for what is to come, in her journey across the sky.

But the path of the just is as the shining light, that shineth more and more unto the perfect day.
Proverbs 4:18

24

Out of nowhere he came

Like a knight he came

With his armor he came

Lifted up I felt

Cleansed I felt

Loved I felt

Joy I felt

Is this what I want?

On my knees I fell

Humbled I fell

Torn I fell

Blessed I fell

Is this what I want?

Joy he gave
Promises he gave
Fulfillment he gave
Peace he gave

Asked, is this what I want?

The spirit, righteousness, truth, peace

I will hear what God the LORD will speak: for he will speak peace unto his people, and to his saints:
but let them not turn again to folly. Surely his salvation is nigh them that fear him; that glory may dwell
in our land. Mercy and truth are met together; righteousness and peace have kissed each other.
Psalms 85:8-10

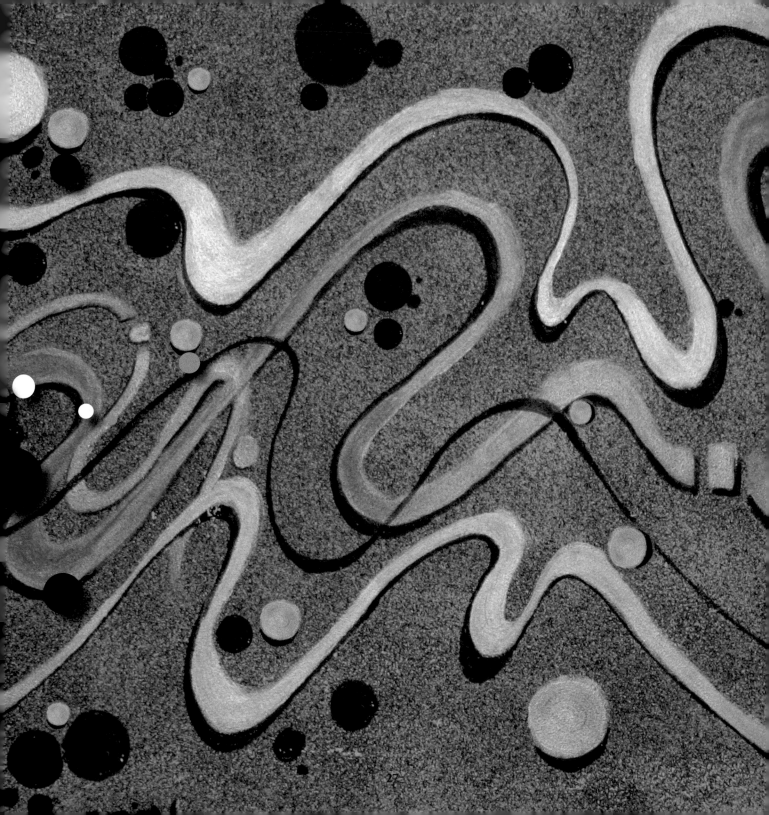

A Journey

Oh what a journey you've taken to come this far. I can't imagine the perils that you've faced, within these rough seas, or the joy you've endured along with your friends.

Oh what a journey you've taken, experiencing the changes in day and night.

The evils and the good of nature's way. The wonders you've seen, in your journey across the sea.

Now you've washed up on my shore, a beauty to behold.

Where you'll face a new journey on the sea shore.
I hope you enjoy it for I'm here to guide you.
Your friends you'll miss but renewed you'll be

living life on the sea shore.

And I will bring the blind by a way that they knew not; I will lead them in paths that they have not known: I will make darkness light before them, and crooked things straight. These things will I do unto them, and not forsake them.
Isaiah 42:16

An Educator

Walks, talks and moves fast A motivator an exciting innovator.

Shows passion, dedication and love.

When explaining they give gestures,

that makes it impossible for you not to understand.

But don't worry if you don't get it, they're available
on or offline excited and ready to help.

They pay great attention to detail, teaching students
how important it is to do so with their great wisdom.

They certainly lead you to the threshold of your own mind.
So it would be sinfully dangerous not to take advantage of their enormous talent and kindness.

The fear of the LORD is the beginning of knowledge: but fools despise wisdom and instruction.
Proverbs 1:7

ack Histo

alcom X

Martin Luth

riet Tubman

Rosa Parks

k T. Washint

We
N
WH

3:
Ma

31

The Messenger

Put on the whole armour of God, that ye may be able to stand against the wiles of the devil. For we wrestle not against flesh and blood, but against principalities, against powers, against the rulers of the darkness of this world, against spiritual wickedness in high places. Wherefore take unto you the whole armour of God, that ye may be able to withstand in the evil day, and having done all, to stand. Stand therefore, having your loins girt about with truth, and having on the breastplate of righteousness; And your feet shod with the preparation of the gospel of peace; Above all, taking the shield of faith, wherewith ye shall be able to quench all the fiery darts of the wicked. And take the helmet of salvation, and the sword of the Spirit, which is the word of God; Praying always with all prayer and supplication in the Spirit, and watching thereunto with all perseverance and supplication of all saints.
Ephesians 6:11-18

I got up at 6 am as I had proposed, to attend the 7:30 am service. I was running late as always, but determined as ever. I entered the parking lot at 7:30 am, surprised to see it full on a rainy day. This man must be important I thought.

As I entered his house I felt safe. Your guides ushered me to my seat. I sat and said a brief prayer for guidance, answers and blessings. I filled out my offering envelope, and was overcome by the choir.

Not knowing what to expect I stood up, a strange soothing sound came bellowing from the altar. My body was not my own, the words cleansed and opened a passage to receive the message. I was transfixed, with my eyes closed and arms raised. I engrossed myself in the message I was about to hear.

My head was bowed in humility because I had decided to come as I am, and be accepted after all these months. Fear, fear of not being accepted, having nothing to offer. Not searching to find the correct answers in the right places.

As I raised my head there he was, a small man, not frightening but inviting. He entered and said a brief prayer quietly. I would propose to ask for guidance and thanking God for using him as a messenger.

He then began to speak softly, as if speaking to a loved one. Announcing of his upcoming marriage,

his flock was ecstatic and he in return thanked them for their many prayers in getting to this point and asked that they continue to do so.

The mood then changes, he begins to teach on the importance of praying. He makes several points on how important it is by backing up his words with passages from the scripture.

His gestures, passion and belief in the word, surely made it impossible for one not to be totally enthralled and become a believer also.

This small man became a king among men. His flock soaked up every word, they gave feedback to nourish his spirit when he exclaimed, "Pray, pray continuously". When he was done he seemed more revived, certain calm came over him. He ended with one coming to the altar pledging her commitment to join and promote the word of God in kind.

I left fulfilled knowing that my prayers were answered. Resolved that I should pray, pray continuously using the full armor of God, praying unselfishly. Just pray all the time in the right way you'll find your answer.

I also left with the promise that I would continue to be faithful.

Releasing all to one true God and believing in his word. Thank you for allowing yourself to be used.

Hadiya

I am God's gift
A magnificent soul.

I groove to the inspirational sounds of my father's tone.

My heritage is that of Swahili.

My variations Hadiyah and Hadiyyah, are Arabic.

I am that gift you seek, your guide to
righteousness.

For by grace are ye saved through faith; and that not of yourselves: it is the gift of God:
Ephesians 2:8

Khadiyah

Behold my essence, my sheer iridescent quality.

I encompass the beauty of an exceptional princess.

My heritage is Arabic or you may see me evolve as Swahili center stage as

a dynamic female.

Who can find a virtuous woman? For her price is far above rubies.
Proverbs 31:10

I am pure love. Experience my exuberant nature, my adorable
charm will lighten your life.

My smile will capture your spirit, for I am filled
with an abundance of love.

Rejoice when you see me for I am not faux but real.

My origins are by the way of Japan.
My presence is lasting.

The statues of the LORD are right, rejoicing the heart: the commandment of the
LORD is pure, enlightening the eyes.
Psalms 19:8

39

My Song

At times I sit and reminisce of the little things I miss
like hugs, and kisses and family dishes.

Everyone playing their own song and living by their own dream.

Now I am playing mine, writing my own lyrics,
laying my own plan, making new memories.
While playing my Song

with my father and I, for he leads the
way as I follow each day.

The LORD is my strength and song, and he is become my salvation: he is my God, and I will prepare
him a habitation; my father's God, and I will exalt him.
Exodus 15:2

41

Burdens

We sometimes wonder why do we choose to carry such heavy loads.

Are we chosen to carry out such tasks?

Is it our destiny?

The path is narrow, I know he's there.
The road is rough, I know he's there.
I've seen how he works, he carries me along the road.

He enlightens me, he allows me to take charge.

As I look above I see the horizons.

I see a new day has come those burdens are now challenges.

Those burdens a goal to complete, a task to accomplish.

A gift to make me stronger, a show to make me wiser.

Cast thy burden upon the LORD, and he shall sustain thee: he shall
never suffer the righteous to be moved
Psalms 55:22

43

fog

You may think that

I am here to confuse you, to blind you.

Look carefully in the mist there is a light

to lead you out

and when it clears, you will see things in a renewed spirit.

Allowing you to be fulfilled and

lightened to start again.

Shine within that light

and watch that fog dissipate.

Yet a little while is the light with you. Walk while ye have the light, lest darkness come upon you: for he that walketh in darkness knoweth not whither he goeth. While ye have light, believe in the light, that ye may be the children of light.
John 12:35-36

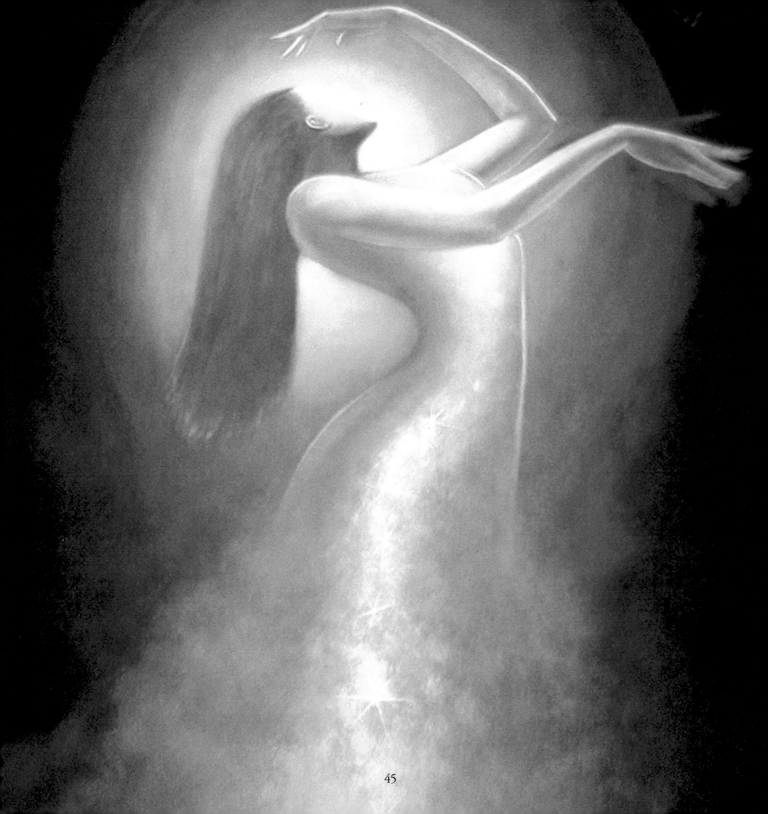

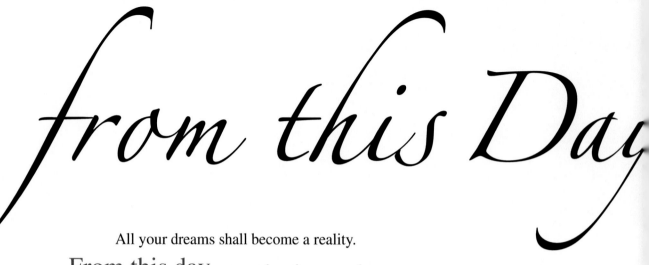

All your dreams shall become a reality.

From this day on your love is renewed.

From this day on your souls will share a common tread.

From this day on forevermore shall be your mantra.

Together you shall be until eternity.

Let no one disturb your togetherness.

Allow yourself to grow,
for it only enhances your soul.

Remove all temptations allow your spirits to guide you.

Cherish each dance that joyous
dance to the sounds of heaven.

Likewise, ye husbands, dwell with them according to knowledge, giving honour unto the wife, as unto
the weaker vessel, and as being heirs together of the grace of life; that your prayers be not hindered.
1 Peter 3:7

Precious Moments

Remember proper execution will bring success.

Self discipline is a must.
Directions hold the proper stance,
take a stand.

Yet still be humble against the struggle
give them no excuse.

The mission comes first, my people take heed.

To succeed you must rehearse

for precious moments like these.

Humble yourselves therefore under the mighty hand of God,
that he may exalt you in due time.
1 Peter 5:6

At Times

I can feel you
wrapping your arms around me.
At times I can feel your

spirit running through me.
At times I can feel you
guiding me by the hand.

At times I can feel your warm tender kiss.

At times I can feel you
inside, warm and at home.
At times I can feel you entering that zone.

At times I can feel you and you're not
even there. At times I can feel you

Everywhere.

God is our refuge and strength, a very present help in trouble.
Psalms 46:1

It's Ok

To feel safe, loved It's ok to wonder how long this will last.

I thank him for being here, for caring, sharing for he didn't have to.
I weep because I'm grateful.

I weep because I'm safe.

It's ok to wonder how long this will last.

revel in his presence.

My mind fantasizes about a near future.

My soul is at a stand still, I want to feel protected loved, wanted, secured.

It's ok to wonder how long it will last.

In his care there's no need to wonder, just allow him and he'll be there.

Cast thy burden upon the Lord, and he shall sustain thee; he shall
never suffer the righteous to be moved.
Psalms 55:22

Grace

Peace and bountiful joy will always be with you.

As I meditate I find within a path of love.

It may not be with you now but just stay still, continue in your faith
for it is all we have in our times of struggle.

Soon you will see that light, let there
be no doubt your desires are near. For this will pass

Appreciate all the gifts around you,

for every day and everyone has a gift to share.

Allow each moment to encompass your soul for
your presence is irresistible.

Therefore I say unto you, Take no thought for your life, What ye
shall eat, or what ye shall drink; nor yet for your body, what ye shall put on.
Matthew 6:25

The Answer

He is my needs answered.

When I am silent my heart listens.
All thoughts, desires, expectations are born and shared with joy.

My passions, pleasures, sorrows
are part of his spirit that allows

my soul to soar, creating new life.
And in his presence

my love becomes clearer, stronger.
I will sing, dance and be joyous, for only life can play the strings of music

to which I dance, forevermore.

Who satisfieth thy mouth with good things; so that thy youth is renewed like the eagle's.
Psalms 103:5

Jonquille

Jonquille grew up in a small village in Guyana, called Sheet Anchor. She has two younger siblings and is the mother of two girls. Jonquille was raised by her Grandmother Mummy Iris, her many aunts, uncles and neighbors. When she was a young girl her parents migrated to the United States. Jonquille started writing her emotions on paper at the age of nine. At the age of ten Jonquille and her two younger brothers joined their parents in the Bronx. Jonquille's first book was "Oh What a Journey" published in 2003, available on Xlibris. com/OhWhatAJourney.html. This is her second book in growth; she now resides in Atlanta, Georgia with her family. Writing has always been a passion of hers.

Contact: jonquille1@juno.com
www.emotionalenegery.us

Deion George

Graphic Designer in New Jersey designed: cover layout, Seasons, Hadiya and On the Path.
Contact: www.deiongeorge.com

H. Mulgrave

Jamaican artist, painted "I Am" image.

Lonnie Ollivierre

Painter: born in St Vincent, painted: Dazzling, It's Ok, Fog, Educator, Sister-Friend, Kiora, The Answer, Offerings, Sunrise, Khadiyah, Precious moments, At Times, Journey, From This Day and Eze. *Contact: www.lonnieostudio.com*

Errol Tomlinson

Painter: born in Jamaica, painted: Burdens, Father & Son, My Song, Grace, Precious moments in time.
Contact: eftomlinson@comcast.net

Tyrone Shorter

Graphic Designer, created "Rain" in collaboration with Deion George.

Mission

Our mission is to energize each and every spirit by providing encouraging words and pieces of art to all.